START-UP
RELIGION

VISITING A SYNAGOGUE

Ruth Nason

Evans

Published by Evans Brothers Limited
2A Portman Mansions
Chiltern Street
London W1U 6NR

© Evans Brothers Limited 2005

Produced for Evans Brothers Limited by
White-Thomson Publishing Ltd,
Bridgewater Business Centre,
210 High Street,
Lewes, East Sussex BN7 2NH

Printed in China by WKT Co. Ltd.

Consultants: Jean Mead, Senior Lecturer in Religious
Education, School of Education, University of
Hertfordshire; Dr Anne Punter, Partnership Tutor,
School of Education, University of Hertfordshire.
Designer: Carole Binding

Cover: All photographs by Chris Fairclough

British Library Cataloguing in Publication Data
Nason, Ruth
    Visiting a synagogue - (Start-up religion)
    1. Public worship - Judaism - Juvenile literature
    2. Synagogues - Juvenile literature
    I. Title
    296'4

ISBN: 0 237 527685

Acknowledgements:
Special thanks to the following for their help and
involvement in the preparation of this book: the
Skillman family, the Wise family, Lana Young, and
other members of the congregation of the Radlett
and Bushey Reform Synagogue.

Picture Acknowledgements:
Art Directors/TRIP: page 21 (S. Shapiro); Corbis:
page 14 (Tim Page); World Religions Photo
Library: page 4 (bottom).
All other photographs by Chris Fairclough.

Pictures of the synagogue are of simulations and
were not photographed during Holy days.

Contents

What is a synagogue?

A synagogue is a building where Jewish people meet and worship God. Sometimes they call the synagogue the shul.

▶ They go to classes there to learn about the Jewish religion.

◀ Sometimes they have parties at the synagogue.

synagogue   Jewish   worship   God

▼ On Saturdays, many Jewish people go to a service at the synagogue.

At a service, people say prayers from a prayer book. What are some of these people wearing around their shoulders?

Do you know what this man is carrying? (See page 6.)

shul   religion   service   prayers   5

The Torah scrolls

▶ The man is carrying a scroll, inside a velvet cover.

▼ Inside the scroll are the words of the Torah, the Jewish holy book. It is written in Hebrew.

For Jewish people, the Torah is the most precious thing in the synagogue.

► Most synagogues have several Torah scrolls. In a service, one of them is carried around the synagogue. People reach out to touch it, to show that they love the Torah.

◄ Later, children help to take the cover off the Torah scroll. Then the scroll is taken to the **reading desk** and opened.

Hebrew   precious   reading desk   **7**

Reading the Torah

▶ Reading aloud from the Torah, in a service, is a very special task. Joshua is using a pointer called a **yad** to follow the words.

◀ After the reading, someone holds the Torah scroll high, for everyone at the service to see.

yad

► At home, Samuel and Rebecca have picture books of stories from the Torah. One is about Noah's Ark.

◄ Another story is about Joseph and his coat of many colours.

Many Jewish people say that the stories in the Torah teach them how to behave well towards one another.

Noah's Ark   Joseph   behave   9

Laws in the Torah

There are many laws in the Torah, as well as stories. The Torah says that God gave the laws to the Jewish people.

◄ Some synagogues have pictures like this of the most famous laws, called the Ten Commandments. The Hebrew letters stand for the numbers 1 to 10.

laws   Commandments

All God's laws for the Jewish people are in the Torah.

▶ One law is: "Show **respect** for old people and **honour** them."

◀ Another law is: "Do not lie or cheat."

When do you think these laws would help you to know what to do?

respect   **honour**

Shabbat

One of the Ten Commandments is: "Keep the seventh day of the week holy, for God." In Hebrew, the seventh day is called Shabbat. It starts on Friday at sunset and ends on Saturday evening.

▲ On Friday evenings, Jewish families light two Shabbat candles.

▲ They eat a meal together, and sing Shabbat songs.

holy   Shabbat   candles

On Saturday mornings people go to the Shabbat service at the synagogue.

▶ Joshua and Ethan take their prayer books and prayer shawls with them, in special bags.

◀ All Jewish men wear prayer shawls for services. Some women and boys wear them too.

prayer shawls

Loving the Torah

Jewish people love the Torah because they believe that God gave it to them. They look after it in special ways.

◄ A Torah scroll is always **handwritten** in Hebrew by a **scribe**. What has this scribe used to write with?

handwritten   scribe

► When people read from a Torah scroll, they do not touch the writing. They use a yad to follow the words.

◄ Beautiful covers are made for the Torah scrolls.

◄ Some of the scrolls have bells on top. They jingle as the scroll is carried around the synagogue.

bells

A school visit

If you visit a synagogue, you will see the special place where the Torah scrolls are kept. It is called the Ark.

► You will also see the reading desk where the scrolls are opened and read.

Ark

If you are a boy, you may be asked to wear a kippah on your head. Jewish men and boys always wear a kippah in the synagogue, to show respect for God.

What else do you think all visitors can do, to show respect in the synagogue?

kippah

The Ark

The Ark is the most important part of the synagogue. All the people at a service sit facing the Ark.

▶ At special times in a service, the Ark is opened, so that everyone can see the Torah scrolls.

What happens to one of the Torah scrolls in a service? Look back at pages 7 and 8.

▶ At the end of the service, the scroll is closed and covered and carried back to the Ark.

◀ A light called the ner tamid hangs above the Ark. It is never turned off. This shows the idea that God is always there.

ner tamid

What have you learnt?

Here are some things that you may see when you visit a synagogue. Can you remember what they are called and what they are for?

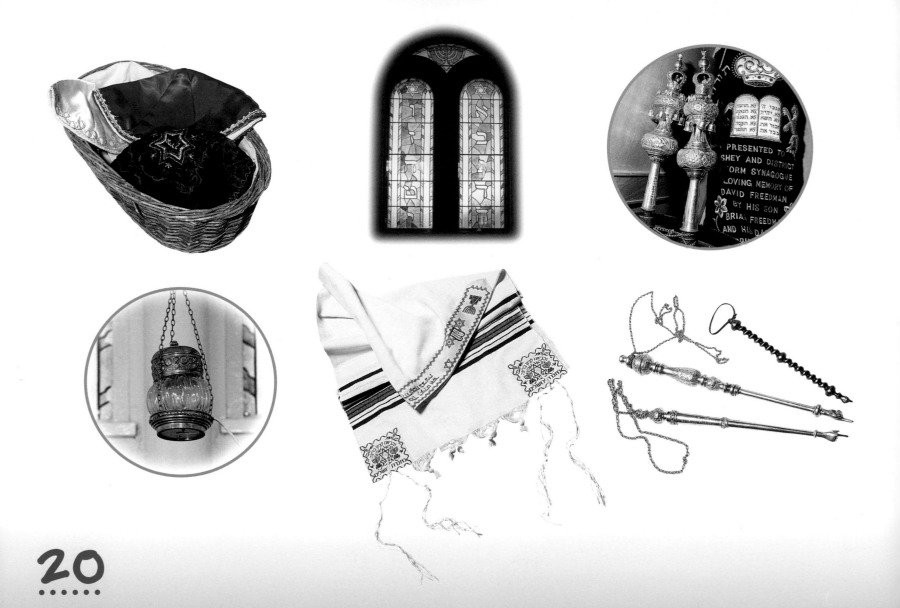

Do you remember some ways in which Jewish people show that they love their holy book, the Torah?

A part of the Torah is read in the synagogue every Shabbat. In the autumn, a day comes when the last part is read. Then the Torah scroll is wound back to the beginning and the first part is read too. This day is called Simhat Torah.

▶ On Simhat Torah, all the Torah scrolls are carried around the synagogue, and the children wave flags. What pictures can you see on this flag?

Simhat Torah

Further information for

Background Information

The Jewish religion dates back to biblical times, but is a living, diverse religion in the 'here and now'. The synagogue featured in this book belongs to the Reform movement within Judaism. Care has been taken not to offend the Orthodox Jewish community, but the practices, and particularly the attitude towards interpretation of the *Torah*, may differ in some aspects. Teachers should try to show, by example, respect for both traditional and more liberal beliefs and practices, without going into complicated explanations with such young children.

The *Torah* contains the first five books of the Bible. It is often translated as 'The Law', although it contains stories with moral teachings as well as instructions. Teachers should try to avoid giving the derogatory impression that Jewish interpretation is 'legalistic'. E.g. 'an eye for an eye' is interpreted in Rabbinic debate as requiring equivalent compensation for injury or loss. The practices involved in observing some laws may seem illogical to outsiders, but as the motivation for obedience is love and reverence for God, teachers should take care not to describe them with amusement.

'The Hebrew Bible' is the preferred term to use for what Christians (but not Jews) call 'The Old Testament'.

Pages 4-5: *Shul* means 'school'. The prayer book (*siddur*) referred to is in Hebrew and English. Some people are wearing a prayer shawl (*tallit*) and skullcap (*kippah*).

Page 10: The ten Hebrew letters on the stained-glass window are the numbers 1-10 and represent the Ten Commandments. Some synagogues use the first word of each commandment.

Page 11: The laws referred to are from Leviticus 19.11 and 32. The Ten Commandments are in Exodus 20.

Page 19: The *ner tamid* is a reminder of the *menorah* lamp in the Temple, signifying the everlasting presence of God.

Suggested Activities

PAGES 4-5
Talk about places of worship and discuss what people do there (e.g. Sunday School, madrasah, clubs, festivals, weddings, as well as worship and prayer). Discuss the value of community meeting places.
Invite a Jewish visitor, or show real artefacts as in the picture.

Parents and Teachers

PAGES 6-7

Talk about things that are 'precious' to us.

Make a display about the class's special books, with labels telling why they were chosen.

Show how a miniature Torah scroll is rolled and read, or make a model to demonstrate.

PAGES 8-9

Show video clips of children reading or learning Hebrew. It is read from right to left. Let children practise writing some Hebrew letters, for example their own initial.

Appreciate any children who know more than one language. Show picture books of stories from the Torah. Discuss what they can teach people.

PAGES 10-11

Tell the story of the Ten Commandments (Exodus 19 and 20). Use or write a children's version of the commandments.

Let a group of children try playing a game without knowing the rules, then discuss the value of rules, in games, in school, in life. Make a display of class rules.

PAGES 12-13

Discuss the meaning of 'holy' as special for God and list the 'holy' items in the book.

Sort comparable items into 'ordinary' and 'special' (e.g. a scarf/prayer shawl).

Relate special clothes to particular activities.

PAGES 14-15

Write a poem about a most precious thing in 'best' hand-writing onto a scroll.

Discuss ways of showing love of a book.

Imagine an invitation from the Queen being both physically treasured and its content acted on.

PAGES 16-17

Plan a visit to a synagogue or use a 'virtual visit'. Discuss ways of behaving appropriately in a range of buildings.

PAGES 18-19

Make a plan of a synagogue visited and put cut-out pictures of items in their correct places. Discuss how we can work out what is important to the people who worship there.

Think about the use of light and the way it makes us feel.

PAGES 20-21

In literacy, when you have finished a book, celebrate books with a 'parade' (holding books and waving decorated flags?).

Write appreciation letters to authors.

Look at pictures or video clips of *Simhat Torah*.

Roll a miniature scroll right to the end and then rewind it to the beginning. Are books easier to manage?

Index